THE ISSA MANUSCRIPT

An American Public Policy Statement

Metadata

Title: The ISSA Manuscript: An American Public Policy Statement

Type: Non-Fiction Paperback

Category: General/Trade

Author: Scott A Ginn

Trim Size: 6 x 9 inch

Page Count: 45

Price: $12.99

Book Description:

As a major Entitlement program, Social Security has been neglected to the brink of insolvency. The ISSA Manuscript is a Public Policy Statement regarding the funding and actuarial status of future Social Security Trust Funds. It is a 'financial blueprint' of how Privatized Social Security Accounts could work in the United States; many factors that should be considered, and why they are needed. Over the years, this book has been revised many times. A Former Stockbroker authored this book; it was researched, proofread, and mailed directly to Congressional lawmakers, Government officials, and Public Policy experts over a 10-year time span (from July 2010 to July 2020).

BISAC Codes

1. POL027000 Political Science/Public Policy/Social Security
2. BUS029000 Business & Economics/Free Enterprise & Capitalism
3. BUS050040 Business & Economics/Personal Finance/Retirement Planning

Keywords and Phrases

Social Security; Privatization; Public Policy; Conservatism; Retirement

THE ISSA MANUSCRIPT

An American Public Policy Statement

Scott A Ginn

A Non-Fiction Book

The ISSA Manuscript: An American Public Policy Statement

Copyright © 2021 Scott A Ginn.

ISSA Account℠ Pending 2021

Publisher's Cataloging-in-Publication data

Names: Ginn, Scott A., author.
Title: The ISSA manuscript: an American public policy statement / author: Scott A. Ginn.
Description: Phoenix, AZ: Gen X Books, 2022.
Identifiers: LCCN: 2022903455 | ISBN: 978-0-578-32837-9 (paperback) | 978-0-578-29562-6 (ebook)
Subjects: LCSH International Social Security Association. | Social security—United States. | Retirement income—Planning. | Finance, Personal. | BISAC POLITICAL SCIENCE / Public Policy / Social Security | BUSINESS & ECONOMICS / Free Enterprise & Capitalism | BUSINESS & ECONOMICS / Personal Finance / Retirement Planning
Classification: LCC HD7090 .G56 2022 | DDC 368.4--dc23

ISBN Paperback: 978-0-578-32837-9
ISBN eBook: 978-0-578-29562-6

Library of Congress Control Number: 2022903455

Publisher: Gen X Books (June 30, 2022)

Printed in the USA

TABLE OF CONTENTS

PREFACE

I didn't intend to write a book; it just worked out that way. Let me start from the beginning. Back in Northern California in the late 1980s, at a weekend keg party with friends, a political discussion about Social Security was brought up. At that time, my Generation X peers were already convinced that Baby Boomers would "suck Social Security dry," leaving little (if anything) for future generations. I didn't think that was fair, and I never forgot it for some reason. I would graduate from college with a Bachelor of Arts degree in Political Science, would later become a licensed Stockbroker, and complete some coursework in pursuit of the Certified Financial Planner designation.

Former President George W Bush attempted the Full Privatization of Social Security back in 2005. When his efforts failed, I thought to myself, in frustration: "I could do a better job." So in July of 2010, while the Tea Party Movement was at its height, I started writing. And researching. This book is the result of those efforts. By studying how Social Security privatization worked in other countries, I carefully developed a plan and concluded that a partial privatization model might work best here in the United States. I knew that it wouldn't be easy. To my surprise, my manuscript had begun as a Keynesian demand-side economic business plan. But I couldn't make it work.

However, only by switching economic theories did I grasp that a supply-side economic business plan, otherwise known as "Trickle-down economics," would work. Although my best efforts may not be good enough, I continued writing, nonetheless.

I kept writing mainly because no one else was even trying to fix Social Security. It is widely known that Social Security is considered the "electric third-rail" of politics to elected lawmakers. Both parties (Republicans and Democrats) are wary of changing the popular Entitlement program. I'm afraid I have to disagree with them. Congress has a 20th-century mentality for a 21st-century problem. Absent major changes to the program, the Social Security Administration will have no choice but to significantly reduce benefits to future generations. To me, the looming insolvency of Social Security trust funds is not a foregone conclusion. This book is a serious discussion about how alternatives, such as Privatized Social Security Accounts, can safeguard and extend the useful life of Social Security for years to come.

January 2021

To Honorable US House Representative Dan Crenshaw (R-TX):

Hello Sir, my name is Scott A Ginn. Enclosed is the finished version of a concept that I've been working on: Privatized Social Security Accounts. After more than 10 calendar years of research, time, and effort, I have completed this project. I cannot improve upon this manuscript in any way; it is my finest work. Therefore, I am sending you this final revision, as I thought that you might want to have an original copy for yourself.

As an Entitlement program, Social Security must modernize; become more useful to future recipients, and be more responsive to the needs of a 21st-century workforce. Three American Generations (Generation X, Millennium Generation, Generation Z) are quite interested in this concept becoming a future Government program. Statistics support this premise; according to a 2011 Pew Research Center study, **69**% of Generation X and **86**% of the Millennium Generation favor Social Security Privatization. By extrapolation (of these figures), our newest American Generation (Generation Z) may support Social Security Privatization in numbers approaching **90**%, overall.

I believe there may be both bipartisan and bicameral support for this endeavor. I would consider the introduction, debate, voting, and passage of this legislation in either Chamber of Congress to be a major accomplishment. I have written all that I can. My contact information has been included; thank you for your time and consideration.

Sincerely,
Scott A Ginn

November 2020

To Honorable Senator Mitch McConnell (R-KY), Senate Majority Leader:

<u>Subject</u>: Social Security Administration

It is my concern that without an alternative, self-directed and market-based solution to safeguard Social Security assets, those aged 50 and under will likely have to work for the rest of their lives, with little confidence that the Social Security system (in its present form) will be solvent for their retirement. In 2011, Congress attempted to begin controlling massive Government spending, which has occurred over the last two decades and continues to this day.

Attached is an elective, after-tax program that would give taxpayers a sense of ownership and self-control over their future retirement assets. My concept is thorough, rooted in academic theory, occupational study (brokerage licensing), and practical work experience gained during my career in the financial services industry. Hopefully, this plan could be adopted to innovate (modernize) how elective Social Security contributions can fund the Social Security system and allow taxpayers to achieve market-based returns in their own Privatized Social Security Accounts.

Cordially,

Scott A Ginn

November 2020

To Dr. Alan Greenspan, Chairman of the Federal Reserve Board of Governors:

Hello Sir, my name is Scott A Ginn. Many years ago, I sent you a 10-page rough draft of a concept I was working on: Privatized Social Security Accounts. After ten (10) calendar years, it is now complete. I wanted to send you the most advanced version of this concept, as it has grown into a comprehensive business plan.

I am writing to you concerning the long-term solvency of the Social Security Administration. In 2018, Social Security trust funds began depleting due to the ongoing retirement of the massive Baby Boomer generation. Conventional wisdom states that there are only four main ways to "fix" Social Security: raise the Social Security (FICA) tax rate; raise the full or normal retirement age, raise the payroll tax ceiling to a higher amount, or cut Social Security retirement benefits **20-25%** for the next generation.

The problem with this last "solution" is that it will directly affect my generation (Generation X) when we reach the full or normal retirement age of 67 in **2035**. There is another alternative: Privatized Social Security Accounts. Ratifying such accounts in the present day would give my generation enough "time" to save tax-free for retirement if future benefit cuts become necessary, or are unavoidable. A simple legislative action plan should help fix Social Security's long-term revenue shortfalls and fiscal problems now through the following small, modest changes:

1. Raise the Social Security (FICA) tax rate from 6.2% to 6.7%, for both employers and employees (combined rates: 12.4% to 13.4%). This tax increase could be phased-in gradually (0.1% per year) over a 5-year period.
2. Raise the full or normal retirement age from 67 years to 68 years.
3. Payroll tax ceiling: No changes to the average wage index or COLA formula(s) based upon the Consumer Price Index for Urban Wage Earners and Clerical Workers, otherwise known as the CPI-W.
4. Authorize the establishment of Privatized Social Security Accounts.

Combining these small changes should reduce (or eliminate) any future benefit cuts and would provide the agency with new revenue stream(s) from brokerage operations not considered before. The enclosed business proposal has taken me 10 years to complete: from July 2010 to July 2020. For full disclosure, mine is a partisan supply-side economic business plan, authored by a lifelong Republican and written as a policy item intended for use by the Republican Party. Five brokerage firms have the adequate scale to run my program: Bank of America/ Merrill Lynch, JP Morgan Chase Bank, Fidelity Investments, Charles Schwab, and TD Ameritrade. All may have an interest in this proposal. With a divided Congress, will it still be possible for my concept to become an actual House or Senate bill to be voted on by Congress? I welcome any questions or feedback regarding this proposal.

Sincerely,
Scott A Ginn

THE ISSA MANUSCRIPT

An American Public Policy Statement

Overview

The Great Recession experienced over the three years (2007-2009) resulted in a significant loss of wealth to many American households. For too long, job losses, loss of equity in a home (market value), or securities (401k account balances, IRA account values) were the norm. While many Americans lost net worth during this period, I contend that a disproportionate amount of financial pain was inflicted upon younger Baby Boomers, Generation X, and the Millennium Generation. These generations have many years, if not decades, of future wage-earning and taxpaying years ahead of them. People in these demographic groups will need unique investments over their remaining working years to support future retirement plans.

Proposal

Develop a new, elective after-tax investment program that will be secure; have low-cost administrative fees, and contain high-grade investment choices that accumulate wealth and compound earnings over time. After much consideration, the following proposal has been created to structure a program that would allow wage earners to have a separate, dedicated retirement account that they can count on when they retire. A self-directed retirement account that would enable participants to outperform government investment returns through private investments instead. It is recognized that there is some complexity to the proposed program, and legislative action is necessary to implement certain provisions.

Proposed Retirement Account
Independent Social Security Administration
Trust Fund Account (ISSA Account)

As a business plan, neither my premise nor the architecture of this retirement system is simple. Therefore, I will outline my concept here in detail. The ISSA program would not be a pre-tax contribution to a qualified retirement plan, like a 401(k) plan or traditional IRA account. It would be an after-tax program, like contributing to a Roth IRA account or variable annuity program. ISSA funds would be listed as a new and separate withholding category on a wage earner's W-2 forms and paystubs. Human resource and payroll-processing companies (e.g., Automatic Data Processing and Paychex) specializing in small-business operations could process this modification by adding a new W-2 withholding category. Employees would make ISSA Account contributions through an automatic investment program (AIP). Employers would agree to withhold these contributions, accrue cash funds weekly or bi-weekly, and then deposit them directly into the account.

Income from brokerage operations shall become a permanent, new revenue stream for the Social Security Administration and directly support the agency's operations. A money market mutual fund will be necessary to open up an ISSA Account, as a cash fund is required for brokerage account transactions. ISSA Accounts, however, will be free to set up online. ISSA Account holders must be informed of the risks of mutual fund investing and agree to accept such investment risks before any mutual fund exchanges could be executed. A warning screen, computer prompt, and legal disclaimers would need to be created on the ISSA trading platform.

Ownership of ISSA trust fund accounts will be registered under the wage earner's **Social Security Number** only; no joint or minor-trust accounts are offered. Like IRA accounts, no spousal privileges are allowed; ISSA trust fund accounts are dedicated to wage earners only.

In the event of a separation from service (voluntary quit, firing, retirement, or layoff), employees with a 401(k) plan can initiate a direct rollover to a self-directed IRA account. The purpose of an IRA direct rollover is to maintain the **Tax-Deferred** status of those assets. Since the structure of a Privatized Social

Security Account is different from that of 401(k) plans, a detailed agreement between the designated retirement plan sponsor or provider for ISSA Accounts and the Depository Trust & Clearing Corporation (DTCC) would need to be reached regarding account transfers. For an ISSA Account, when an account holder starts a new job with a new employer, elective contributions could begin again; with a uniform menu of plan investments that would not change. Although some ISSA investors will prefer to perform a simple account liquidation upon separation from service, Congress may need to add specific language to this plan to allow future account portability. An ISSA Account would grow on a **Tax-Free** basis, like a Roth IRA account.

ISSA trust fund account holders would not need to fill out IRS Schedule B (Interest and Ordinary Dividends) or IRS Schedule D (Capital Gains and Losses) for income tax purposes. IRS 1099-DIV, 1099-INT, and 1099-OID forms would also not need to be distributed, thereby reducing paperwork. A mutual fund exchange within an ISSA Account would not be a taxable event; the account would function like other qualified retirement plans.

Since ISSA Accounts would be considered nondeductible contributions to a retirement plan (like a Roth IRA account), investors may be able or eligible to qualify for the Retirement Savings Contribution Credit. This is also called the Saver's Tax Credit; a nonrefundable tax credit which may be applied for every tax year. (Current maximum annual tax credits: $1000 for single or head of household; $2000 for married filing jointly). IRS Forms 8606 or 8880 may need to be filled out to qualify. At the discretion of Congress, existing federal and state small-business tax credits may be added to or included within this proposal as an incentive for participating employers who offer this retirement plan (the ISSA Account) to their employees.

No "cost basis" would be necessary to calculate distributions at retirement age for the reasons stated above. Year-end dividends, short-term capital gains, and long-term capital gain distributions (if any) would be reinvested automatically into each specific mutual fund (cannot be redirected or redistributed into other funds).

ISSA Plan Overview and Eligibility Issues

Independent Social Security Administration Trust Fund Accounts (hereafter referred to as ISSA trust fund accounts, the ISSA plan, or an ISSA Account)[SM] are designed for adult US citizen (age 18+) wage earners who have earned income and are paying Social Security taxes; otherwise known as Federal Insurance Contributions Act or FICA taxes.

Since this is a modern account serving the long-term needs of future retirees and Social Security recipients, the maximum cutoff age to open an ISSA Account will be Age 59 ½. Retired individuals (Age 62+) already receiving Social Security retirement benefit payments shall be ineligible to establish an ISSA Account. Business entities requiring a tax identification number (partnerships, corporations, LLCs) will not be eligible to enroll in the ISSA plan, either.

Finally, non-US citizens with an Individual Tax Identification Number (ITIN) shall be ineligible to enroll in the ISSA plan, as well. Small-business payroll cycles, whether weekly or bi-weekly, may not coincide exactly with automatic investments into an ISSA Account, and will be the responsibility of the retirement plan sponsor or provider to invest cash funds received as soon as possible. (Same-day ACH transactions became possible in late 2017. If these money transfers could be applied to the ISSA AIP in the future, I would strongly encourage using this service, even at an additional cost).

The concept itself is simple: incremental mutual fund investing (share-building) over a long period of time. AIP purchases would be transmitted electronically within the ISSA Account to reduce paperwork and record-keeping. Also, this program is a free service; no additional fees or sales charges will apply to purchases. Under an account activity menu, investors could see the date, dollar amount(s), the number of mutual fund shares purchased, and the fund's purchase price (NAV-net asset value). Only mutual fund exchanges would require printed (mailed) or electronic (e-mail) confirmations to comply with stock exchange trading requirements.

The 2010 Tax-Cut Compromise Bill lowered the Social Security tax rate from 6.2% (where it had stood for decades) down to 4.2% (for employees). However, by 2013 the tax rate reverted back to its original level (6.2%). I propose six elective after-tax contribution rates that employers would withhold, accrue weekly or bi-weekly funds, and then invest directly into an employee's ISSA trust fund account. These elective payroll deduction rates would be as follows: 1.0%, 2.0%, 3.0%, 4.0%, 5.0%, or 6.0%. Employees will choose their introductory ISSA contribution rate and make changes after the initial plan enrollment date. Sample rates are listed below.

6.2%-Ordinary FICA taxes deducted
1.0%-Elective ISSA Account contribution
7.2%-Total Social Security deductions

6.2%-Ordinary FICA taxes deducted
2.0%-Elective ISSA Account contribution
8.2%-Total Social Security deductions

6.2%-Ordinary FICA taxes deducted
3.0%-Elective ISSA Account contribution
9.2%-Total Social Security deductions

6.2%-Ordinary FICA taxes deducted
4.0%-Elective ISSA Account contribution
10.2%-Total Social Security deductions

6.2%-Ordinary FICA taxes deducted
5.0%-Elective ISSA Account contribution
11.2%-Total Social Security deductions

6.2%-Ordinary FICA taxes deducted
6.0%-Elective ISSA Account contribution
12.2%-Total Social Security deductions

Divorce Clause

A domestic relations order (DRO) will be required in the event of divorce. A DRO is a court order directing plan administrators to assign all or a portion of a party's retirement benefit to a former spouse. 401(k) plans subject to ERISA rules require a qualified domestic relations order (or QDRO) instead.

Estate and Probate Clause

For estate purposes, upon the death of an ISSA Account holder, the account shall be retitled as an Inherited SSA account, quite similar to an Inherited IRA account. All ISSA trust fund accounts must have beneficiaries listed when the account is opened. (Both primary and secondary beneficiaries will be required).

After receiving notification of an account holder's death, the brokerage firm would request a death certificate, current court letter of appointment, stock power of attorney, or affidavit of domicile. Additional documentation, such as new Social Security Administration or brokerage account form(s), may also be required to transfer ownership and retitle an account as an Inherited SSA account; similar to IRA account regulations.

Mentioned earlier, ISSA Accounts will be named accounts with stated beneficiaries, thereby avoiding future probate proceedings. The requirement(s) of named beneficiaries and long-term plan restrictions should both qualify for and comply with the Uniform Transfer on Death (TOD) Security Registration Act of the Uniform Probate Code.

Related Proposed Legislation

Alongside legislation to create Privatized Social Security Accounts for private sector workers, I would urge Congress to adopt or enact House Resolution 3934: The Equal Treatment of Public Servants Act of 2019, authored by Ranking House Ways and Means Committee Member Kevin Brady (R-TX). This Act would repeal the 1983 Windfall Elimination Provision (WEP) and create a new, modern formula to calculate Social Security benefits for public sector workers and their non-covered earnings.

Institutional Account Guidelines

For purposes of market competition and to prevent potential (or inherent) conflicts of interest, investment companies that offer their mutual funds (as investments) through the ISSA plan may not also serve as the investment bank, transfer agent, or trust company necessary to complete financial transactions, unless specified.

Congress shall determine the future investment bank or brokerage firm used to execute mutual fund exchanges through legislative lobbying efforts. Future ISSA trading platform yet to be decided. No Grandfather clauses or Sunset provisions shall exist for ISSA trust fund accounts; in the year this plan becomes law, wage earners older than age 59 ½ will be ineligible to participate in the ISSA retirement program. This plan was built for Generation X, the Millenium Generation, and Generation Z, who may have many years (if not decades) of future wage-earning and taxpaying years ahead of them and desire more control and greater investment returns on their future retirement assets.

Institutional Account Operations and Structure

The original operational structure of the ISSA program required the federal government to build customer service and data centers at select locations across the country. ISSA was intended to be a specialized division within the Social Security Administration itself; employees would be government agents or contract workers.

Here is the verbatim text for early drafts of the ISSA Account and its operational structure: "A large stock exchange would, most likely, be needed to execute and settle Mutual fund transactions; send out exchange confirmations, and financial record-keeping. My two choices of exchanges: either the NYSE-Euronext Exchange or the NASDAQ-AMEX exchange. For purposes of record-keeping, account identification, and speedy execution of Mutual Fund exchanges, an Omnibus account for ISSA Trust Fund Accounts may need to be established on one of the two exchanges listed. Perhaps the US Treasury Department (itself) could serve as the Custodian/Transfer Agent/ Commercial Bank needed to complete investment transactions."

Future ISSA customers would log in to the MySSA.gov website to perform secure financial transactions. I also considered modifying the annual Social Security statement, which would include year-end values of ISSA Account holdings, with a pie-chart portfolio breakdown by asset class. Over time, I realized this structure's complexity, difficulties, and limitations and changed it.

The ISSA plan should be subcontracted or outsourced to an investment bank or brokerage firm instead since they have the existing infrastructure (local bank branches, regional brokerage houses, customer service and data centers), industry expertise, and resources necessary to run a program as extensive as mine. The federal government would award a long-term contract (**10-year minimum**). Through legislative lobbying efforts, Congress should determine who would become the designated retirement plan sponsor or provider for Privatized Social Security Accounts. I intended to use the agency's MySSA.gov website portal to perform secure financial transactions. Social Security web requirements and restrictions (as of 2018) would not work for this account, so I no longer consider MySSA.gov as a business-friendly web portal for brokerage operations. A private sector website or trading platform would work much better for the ISSA plan. The platform was created in January 2013 (see graphics).

my Social Security
How to Create an Online Account

You can create a *my* Social Security account to access your *Social Security Statement*, check your earnings, and get your benefit estimates.

If you receive benefits, you can also:

- Get your benefit verification letter.
- Change your address and phone number.
- Start or change your direct deposit.
- Request a replacement Medicare card.
- Get a replacement SSA-1099 or SSA-1042S for tax season.
- Opt out of notices available online.

Even if you do not currently receive benefits, you can:

- Check the status of your application or appeal.
- Get a benefit verification letter stating that you:
  - Never received Social Security benefits, Supplemental Security Income (SSI) or Medicare.
  - Received benefits in the past, but do not currently receive them (The letter will include the date your benefits stopped and how much you received that year).
  - Applied for benefits but haven't received a decision yet.

In most states, you can request a replacement Social Security card online using your free, personal *my* Social Security account as long as you are not requesting a name change or any other change to your card, and you meet other requirements.

To create your free, personal *my* Social Security account, you must have a valid email address.

Email account set up

There are many options available to set up an email address and it can be done in as little as five minutes. Each email provider has its own criteria for setting up an account and you must accept the provider's terms of use agreement. Some examples of free email providers include:

AOL: *aolmail.com*

Gmail: *gmail.com*

iCloud Mail (Apple): *icloud.com*

Outlook: *outlook.com*

Yahoo: *yahoo.com*

*This is not a complete list of email providers. Social Security is not endorsing any of these particular email account provider(s), and you may use other email account providers as appropriate.

NOTE: *Even if you do not use email on the computer, if you have a smartphone it is likely that you already have an email account. Contact your cell phone service provider to find out.*

Create your personal *my* Social Security account

To create a *my* Social Security account, you must be at least 18 years old and have:

- A valid email address.
- A Social Security number.
- A U.S. mailing address.

Once you have a valid email address, you are ready to set up your personal *my* Social Security account. Visit **www.ssa.gov/myaccount**, select the "Create an Account" button, then follow the steps below and on the back of this page:

Select "Create New Account"

1. Enter your ZIP code on the next screen.
2. Depending on the state you live in, you will have the option of verifying your identity using your driver's license or state-issued ID. If you want to use your ID select "Yes, I'll try it" and then "Next."
3. Read and agree to the Terms of Service, and select "Next."
4. If you do not want to use your ID to verify your identity, select "No, thanks" and select "Next." Then read and agree to the Terms of Service, and select "Next."
5. If the option to use your ID is not available, you will go straight to the terms of service page. Read and agree to the Terms of Service, and select "Next."

SCOTT A GINN

You must provide some personal information to verify your identity

To complete the verification process, you must provide your:

- Name.
- Social Security number.
- Date of birth.
- Home address.
- Email address.
- Phone number (suggested).

Driver's license or state-issued ID option

If you provided a cell phone number, you will be given the choice to upload a photo or to enter your information manually. If you did not provide a cell phone number, you will only be able to enter your information manually.

Photo Upload:

1. Select the "Request Text Message" button.
2. Select the link in the text message and select "Continue."
3. Take a photo of the front of your driver's license, learner's permit, or state-issued ID and select "Continue."
4. When prompted, take a photo of the back of your driver's license, learner's permit, or state-issued ID and select "Continue."
5. If the upload was successful, you will see the screen with the message, "you have completed the photo capture." Go to the window that you left open before taking the photos and finish setting up your account.

If there is a technical issue uploading your photos, you will receive an alert "Retake photo — select try again." If you are still unable to upload your photos, you will be directed to enter your information manually.

Manual Entry:

1. Enter the type of ID you have (driver's license, learner's permit, or state-issued ID), the issuing state, and the ID number.
2. Enter some financial information to complete the verification.

Answer questions only you would know option

If there were verification issues above or you elected not to use your ID, you will need to answer questions only you should know. In some cases, you may be asked to enter additional financial information to verify your identity.

Using your activation code to finish creating your account

You will receive an activation code to complete the process of creating your personal *my* Social Security account. You will be given the option to select whether to receive your activation code by postal mail, email, or text message if we can verify at least one of those three options.

If you receive your activation code via email or text message then you can finish creating your account right away by using the link in the message. If you receive your code by mail, you will need to go to **www.ssa.gov/myaccount** and select "Finish Setting Up Your Account" once you have received your letter.

Choose a username, password, and create your security questions

Choose a username that is between 8 and 20 characters in length, consisting of letters and numbers only. Once we confirm that your requested username is available, you can then create your password.

Your password must:

- Begin with a letter or number.
- Contain 8 to 64 characters.
- Contain upper and lower case letters.
- Contain numbers.
- Contain symbols (! @ # $ % ^ & *).

To choose your security questions, select one question from each of the three drop-down menus and provide an answer for each selected question. Answers to the questions cannot be the same.

NOTE: *We'll send a one-time security code to your cell phone or to your email address each time you sign in with your username and password. The security code is part of our enhanced security feature to protect your personal information. Keep in mind that your cell phone provider's text message and data rates may apply.*

Securing today and tomorrow

Social Security Administration
Publication No. 05-10540 | ICN 459261 | Unit of Issue — HD (one hundred)
November 2020
my Social Security — How to Create an Online Account
Produced and published at U.S. taxpayer expense

ISSA Plan Enrollments

Gradual enrollment is recommended for the ISSA program. In 2008, according to the Social Security Administration's published statistics, 165 million people worked and paid Social Security taxes. Although the US economy improved in 2018 (10 years later), the Great Recession resulted in a smaller labor pool, as discouraged job-seekers left the workforce. Due to this fact, I have scaled back new account processing estimates to 1,250 per day for several reasons. First, no comprehensive plan for Privatized Social Security Accounts (on this scale) has ever been attempted or implemented before. Second, trying to gauge or estimate future demand for a new retirement account or product is extremely difficult. Third, limiting ISSA plan enrollments to 1,250 per day would allow the plan sponsor to manage brokerage staffing needs more efficiently. In Year 1 of the ISSA plan, about 456,000 new ISSA Accounts could be processed. In Year 2 of the ISSA plan, a target goal of 2,500 new accounts per day (or 912,500) enrollments should be possible.

By Year 3 of the ISSA plan, account registration and processing efficiencies will have been realized, so a target goal of 4,000 new accounts per day (or 1.46 million) enrollments should be possible. In Year 4 of the ISSA plan, a target goal of 6,000 new accounts per day (or 2.19 million) registrations should be possible. In Year 5 of the ISSA plan, processing 7,500 new accounts per day (or about 2.74 million) accounts should be possible. By Year 6 of the ISSA plan, a target goal of 10,000 new accounts per day (or 3.65 million) signups may be possible. Beyond this time frame, account enrollments would be determined by the plan sponsor. New ISSA customers should establish an account in several ways: at a local brokerage branch, through an online web portal, or through their employer at work. Enrollment is free to establish an ISSA Account.

Bankruptcy Clause

The US Bankruptcy Code stipulates bankruptcy proceedings and outlines debtors' rights. It states that an individual debtor is entitled to exempt certain property from bankruptcy filings. One category of property exemptions protects the right to receive Social Security and certain welfare benefits, alimony and support, and certain pension benefits. ISSA trust fund accounts should both qualify for and seek legislative protection from the federal government in the event of a bankruptcy filing so that these accounts are not liquidated, and remain intact and invested until retirement.

Operational Provisions

How would an ISSA Account differ from a 401(k) plan? They would basically differ in several distinct ways. First, a 401(k) account is a pre-tax qualified retirement plan, whose voluntary contributions can reduce a private sector employee's taxable income through earned wages. An ISSA Account, on the other hand, is an after-tax, nondeductible retirement account, similar to a Roth IRA or variable annuity plan. Second, many institutional plans offer employer-matching 401(k) funds as an employment incentive or benefit. No such employer-matching funds are allowed in the ISSA program; only employees can make voluntary contributions into their accounts. The employer is simply a temporary custodian of funds and functions as a conduit between the employee and their federal or national ISSA Account.

Finally, 401(k) plans allow employees to loan or borrow against their portfolio's account value, with the express condition that withdrawn 401(k) funds must be deposited within a certain period. This ordinary 401(k) transaction is also called a hardship withdrawal. No such privileges are offered or allowed in ISSA Accounts. An ISSA Account is not a microloan; there are no loan or "borrowing" provisions for ISSA Accounts. For tax purposes, all withdrawals from an ISSA Account are considered distributions from a qualified retirement plan, like an IRA account. The best term to describe this new retirement account is to classify it as a "Roth-Modified ISSA Account."

Since federal, state, and local income taxes have already been paid (deducted from) contributions to an ISSA Account (funded with after-tax dollars), upon separation from service: the mandatory 20% federal withholding tax on lump-sum distributions shall not apply. Instead, 10% early-withdrawal penalties may apply if the account holder is less than 59 ½ years of age, or the account has been open less than five years. These rules are consistent with existing Roth IRA tax rules.

This account will focus on non-high net worth clients, yet is sophisticated enough to benefit experienced investors. Many investment experts would agree: there is a very large, untapped-market of novice investors, newer workers (The Millenium Generation, Generation Z), and small account/low balance investors who want to participate in the stock market but either lack the discretionary income or experience to do so, and feel overlooked by Wall Street. ISSA trust fund account plan stipulations contained within serve as the "lockbox provision" to preserve and protect Social Security Funds, which Congress and prior Administrations (over the last 35 years) have failed to accomplish.

ISSA Shares and Plan Stipulations

Since the ISSA plan is a blend of different retirement accounts, specific rules shall apply to contributions and distributions. Distributions from an ISSA Account prior to age 59 ½ would be subject to 10% early-withdrawal penalties and taxed at ordinary income rates (specifics to follow). Accounts held and open for less than five years would also be subject to these rules, like a Roth IRA account. One category, however, will be exempt from early-withdrawal penalties: the first-time homebuyer exemption. This provision allows first-time homebuyers to withdraw up to **$10,000** toward purchasing a new home, tax-and penalty-free. This provision should comply with the Taxpayer Relief Act of 1997 enacted by Congress. Since this legislation was ratified 25 years ago, Congress could double the exemption to **$20,000** to better reflect cost-of-living increases and median US home prices in late 2017. The other category concerns qualified higher education expenses, which may be defined as follows: 1) tuition and fees; (2) books; (3) supplies and equipment required for coursework and (4) room and board (if enrolled half-time). For after-tax IRA accounts, I would urge Congress to revise the definition of qualified higher education expenses in IRC Section 529(e)(3) to include: (5) "Existing and outstanding student loans used to fund prior academic study at an eligible educational institution." According to the IRS, an eligible educational institution is defined as "any college, university, vocational or other postsecondary educational institution eligible to participate in the student aid programs administered by the US Department of Education. It includes virtually all accredited public, non-profit and proprietary, profit-making post-secondary institutions." Students receive Form 1098-T as proof of attendance. Student loan interest would remain tax-deductible on federal income tax returns.

Modern Account Parameters

This new account was designed to serve the long-term needs of future retirees and Social Security recipients. ISSA is an online retirement account (system of investing) that requires computer literacy and basic technology usage. Therefore, age 59 ½ will be the maximum cutoff age to open an ISSA Account. Retired individuals (age 62+) already receiving Social Security retirement benefits shall be ineligible to establish an ISSA Account. Further, this account was built to serve those born 1960 and later, whose full or normal retirement age will be age 67. Like the Roth IRA account, the required minimum distribution (RMD) rule shall not apply for an ISSA Account, either.

Taxation of ISSA Contributions and Distributions

As outlined before, principal contributions to an ISSA Account are considered nondeductible, after-tax contributions to a qualified retirement plan, like a Roth IRA account. The ISSA plan shall have two-tiered, simplified distribution ordering rules: (1). principal contributions; and (2). investment earnings. Principal contributions shall be treated as qualified distributions (tax-and penalty-free) upon withdrawal, for tax purposes. In contrast, investment earnings inside an ISSA Account shall be considered non-qualified distributions, subject to 10% early-withdrawal penalties and taxed as ordinary income, as well. These rules stay in effect until account holders reach the age of 59½, when any distributions from an ISSA Account become qualified distributions (tax-and penalty-free) following the tax rules for Roth IRA accounts.

AIP Summary

The ISSA automatic investment program is an integral part of this account and an important function. Once enrolled, an employee decides what percentage (1.0%-6.0%) of their net after-tax weekly (7-day) or bi-weekly (14-day) paycheck should be withheld as an elective payroll deduction. The employer would process this ISSA contribution by sending cash funds (by either bank wire or electronic funds transfer) to the retirement plan sponsor, who would automatically invest those funds promptly. This program is a free service; no additional fees or sales charges will be applied to purchases in an ISSA Account. For bronze-level accounts, account maintenance fees of $32.00 could be charged as a monthly fee. It may also be possible to spread out these fees every quarter: bronze-level ($96.00), silver-level ($84.00), gold-level ($72.00), and platinum-level ($60.00). Such fees could be assessed every 90 days and billed separately from any retirement plan contributions (fees paid in this manner may be tax-deductible).

Terms of Trading

Minimum purchase to buy ISSA shares: $100.00 (any fund, except required money market mutual fund). Traditional sales loads will not be charged on bronze-tier investments, or accounts with a balance of less than $10,000. Instead, purchase fees and redemption fees may apply. Other options will also be available. Fund companies already offer no-load Investor Class shares in various accounts. They will also have the ability to offer Class D Shares, provided they do not carry sales loads. In addition, fund companies may offer Class R Shares (specifically-designed for retirement accounts and currently only available through employer-sponsored plans such as 401(k) and 403(b) plans).

Mutual fund companies will have the ability to determine what share class funds they choose to offer in the plan. Mutual fund shares shall be registered in electronic book-entry form only; no physical shares or certificates shall either exist or be held by the Social Security Administration.

Account holders will be able to place trades in two different ways: as a self-directed online transaction (unsolicited order) or broker-assisted transaction (solicited order). The retirement plan sponsor or provider will collect sales loads on premium asset class mutual funds, regardless of order method. Broker-assisted trades will be available for silver, gold, and platinum-level investors at a $25.00 surcharge per mutual fund exchange. Of this service/sales charge, $20.00 will be credited to the retirement plan sponsor; $5.00 will be credited to the Social Security Administration. This service may also be available for bronze-level investors; a $20.00 surcharge could be divided between the retirement plan sponsor ($15.00) and the government agency ($5.00).

Asset Classes Offered in ISSA Accounts

Fixed Income Funds

1. <u>Domestic money market mutual fund</u>. A cash settlement fund is required for an ISSA Account. The money market mutual fund will have a $1.00 NAV (net asset value) and state the effective 7-day SEC yield.

2. <u>US government bond fund</u> (e.g., USAA Government Securities Fund). Only investment-grade debt. Mixed maturities; short-to-intermediate-term bonds. Treasury bills (less than 1 year), Treasury notes (2-10 year maturities), government agency bonds; short-to-mid-term duration. May invest in Treasury inflation-protected securities (TIPS); short-to-mid-term duration. May own limited investment-grade and high-yield US territory bond issues.

3. <u>Corporate bond fund</u> (e.g., T Rowe Price Corporate Bond Fund). All maturities; only investment-grade (AAA-BBB) bond grades. May own domestic and foreign investment-grade corporate debt obligations and limited high-yield domestic corporate bonds.

4. <u>Total bond market fund</u> (e.g., PIMCO Total Return Bond Fund). Invests in the total US bond market and holds three major categories of debt: US Treasury and government agency bonds, corporate bonds, and municipal bond holdings. Must be only investment-grade issues.

A bond "fund of funds" or bond index fund is acceptable. May own limited investment grade foreign government debt obligations and Treasury inflation-protected securities (TIPS). May also own limited investment-grade and high-yield US territory bond issues.

Equity Funds

In terms of guidelines on equity fund holdings, the ISSA plan was designed as an incremental-investing and long-term retirement program which could gain (or lose) value over time. ISSA investors can invest all of their elective, after-tax contributions into fixed income and balanced funds with moderate risk and no additional fund fees. Equity mutual funds are listed below.

5.   Balanced mutual fund (e.g., Merrill Lynch Balanced Fund).
     60%-Equities (S&P 500 large-cap stocks)
     30%-Fixed Income (bonds)
     10%-Cash and Equivalents (Treasury bills, commercial paper, etc.)

6.   Utilities sector fund (e.g., Franklin-Templeton Utilities Fund).
     Stocks that own, operate, or invest primarily in US public and private utilities (electric, gas, and water companies), including oil pipelines, rural railroads, and urban transportation projects. The fund may include energy generation, transport and storage companies, and limited telecom providers (70-85%); Multi-cap value dividend income fund.

7.   Real estate sector fund (e.g., Fidelity Real Estate Fund)
     Stocks that own, operate, or invest in commercial and residential real estate in the United States and US territories (90-100%). REIT index fund is acceptable.

8.   S&P 500 index fund (e.g., Nationwide S&P 500 Index Fund)
     The S&P 500 index is a market cap-weighted index of the 500 largest US publicly-traded companies and is considered an investment benchmark of large-cap stocks. It is one of the best representations of the overall US stock market.

9.   SRI-ESG fund (e.g., Northern Trust US Quality ESG Fund)
     Fund strategy: socially-responsible investing and environmental, social and governance stocks. Multi-cap blend; actively-managed (not an index fund).

10. <u>Mid-cap equity blend fund</u> (e.g., BlackRock Mid-Cap Equity Index Fund) US mid-cap growth and value stocks. Actively-managed mid-cap funds or mid-cap index funds are acceptable (90-100%). Morningstar mid-cap blend category.

11. <u>Diversified small-cap equity blend fund</u> (e.g., USAA Small-Cap Stock Fund) Actively-managed US small-cap core (growth and value) stocks only (90-100%). Similar diversified funds should match Morningstar small-cap blend category.

10 Eligible No-Load Mutual Fund Companies

1. American Funds	6. Nationwide Funds
2. BlackRock Funds	7. Northern Trust Funds
3. Fidelity Funds	8. PIMCO Bond Funds
4. Franklin-Templeton Funds	9. T Rowe Price Funds
5. MFS Funds	10. USAA Group Funds

These 10 (pre-screened) investment companies already offer no-load mutual funds to retail investors in all 11 asset classes (categories) previously listed. Participating mutual fund companies would be required to drop any sales loads on offered mutual funds. The following types of investments will not be offered in the ISSA program: no 'Life-Cycle' or Target-Date Retirement Funds, precious metals sector funds, and leveraged or inverse investments. A menu of diversified or sector exchange-traded funds (ETFs) may be allowed to platinum-level investors only, at the discretion of the investment bank or brokerage firm. This plan is a sophisticated, elective retirement program. Funds may gain (or lose) value over time. Mutual fund companies may offer a maximum of 1 fund per asset class. The secondary mutual fund offering (index fund) must contain the same market-cap or type of securities, with a blended or diversified mutual fund style or emphasis. For instance, T Rowe Price, Fidelity Investments, and BlackRock Funds all offer actively-managed mid-cap stock funds, as well as S&P 400 mid-cap stock index funds. Either fund type could be offered.

Government Agency Agreements or Waivers

Agreements with or waivers from the following government agencies would most likely be necessary: the Securities and Exchange Commission (SEC), Social Security Administration (SSA), and Small Business Administration (SBA). The US Treasury Department and Internal Revenue Service (IRS) comply with Congressional directives. The Department of Labor (DOL) and Department of Education (ED) could help to streamline ISSA plan functions. Since an ISSA Account will contain mutual funds as investments, insurance coverage by the Federal Deposit Insurance Corporation (FDIC) or Securities Investor Protection Corporation (SIPC) is recommended.

Plan Risk-Reduction Methods and Portfolio Theory

From an investment risk perspective, I have devised four built-in methods of reducing investment risk within an ISSA Account while maintaining tax-free status.

1. Limiting inherent securities risk of mutual funds (asset classes) offered in the ISSA plan. All 11 basic bronze-level investments (asset classes) are suitable investments for investors with varied risk tolerance. Asset classes are listed (ranked) by investment risk (lowest to highest). Premium investments require higher account balances.

2. Setting a cap (limit) on free annual mutual fund exchanges and charging fees for extra or additional trading should limit ISSA Account portfolio turnover and reduce costs. The ISSA plan is designed for long-term incremental and diversified mutual fund investing, with limited trading.

3. Identifying risk in an investment portfolio. Four ISSA asset classes are higher-risk investments for two main reasons: market capitalization and liquidity. These funds and their stock holdings trade far less frequently (in daily volume) than large-cap stocks. In addition, the real estate and utilities funds are non-diversified (sector) funds whose performance is closely-correlated to a fall (or rise) in interest rates or commodity prices and may experience volatile price swings. The two smaller-capitalization categories (mid-cap equity blend fund and

diversified small-cap equity blend fund) may experience large inflows of cash during Bull Markets, but also quick and severe outflows of capital (mutual fund redemptions) during Bear Markets. This makes it more difficult for fund managers to operate their funds and invest strategically in volatile market conditions.

4. Allowing purchase fees and redemption fees on basic asset classes. Such fees sound a lot like sales charges (loads), but are paid entirely to the fund, not a broker. The four asset classes listed above, plus the SRI-ESG fund, may levy maximum purchase fees of 2% and maximum redemption fees of 2% on mutual fund exchanges. For the S&P 500 index fund, fund companies may charge maximum purchase fees of no more than 1%, and redemption fees of no more than 1%, on transactions. (All 3 bond mutual funds may levy the same 1% fees, as stated above).

Investment Analysis and Investor Sentiment

Why not include the Wilshire 5000 total stock market index fund, for example, as a basic (bronze-level) investment option? My reasoning is simple. Passive equity index funds match stock market losses as well as stock market gains, depending upon market conditions. Unfortunately, not all investors pay close attention to the stock market or know how their investments are performing, in general. Some investors may not know their actual risk tolerance; others may be short-term (rather than long-term) investors. These assertions are based upon several years of direct knowledge and experience, working as a Registered Representative in the financial services and brokerage industry.

I hold a Bachelor of Arts degree in Political Science from California State University, Chico, with an emphasis in pre-law studies. In addition, I have held three brokerage licenses (FINRA Series 6, 7 & 63) earned through a professional work-study program, and awarded by the same brokerage firm while employed there (1998-2001). Finally, I have taken exams and some coursework towards attaining the Certified Financial Planner (CFP) designation.

In my professional opinion, actively-managed or blended mutual funds should be offered, which can adjust to fluctuating stock market conditions. On a risk/reward basis, however, 5 of 11 asset classes could be offered as bronze-level index funds: the total bond market index fund, utilities index fund, real estate investment trust fund (REIT index), S&P 500 index fund, and S&P 400 midcap index funds. All 10 mutual fund companies listed previously already offer these index funds to retail investors.

Prohibited Contributions and Transactions

The financial services industry has many overlapping rules and regulations stipulating how institutions handle cash transactions, demand deposits (checking accounts), retirement accounts, credit card transactions, and individual securities. Therefore, all five categories are prohibited methods of contributing to an ISSA Account. Attempted contributions of these types will be promptly mailed back to the prospective customer (with explanation) in a postage-paid envelope.

For instance, no cash contributions are allowed. This includes cash, bank savings accounts, money orders, traveler's checks, or certified bank checks. No demand deposits are allowed, either. This includes personal checking accounts (bank checks), money market mutual fund drafts, or bank certificates of deposit. Further, no retirement accounts can be rolled over or merged into an ISSA Account. These include, but are not limited to, the following: Education IRAs, 401(k) plans, 403(b) plans, traditional IRAs, SEP-IRAs, SIMPLE IRAs, or Roth 401(k) plans. Also, credit card contributions are not allowed. These include credit card (cash advances) or debit card transactions. Finally, physical securities cannot be deposited into an ISSA Account. These include stock and bond certificates, US savings bonds (any type), fixed annuities, or variable annuity plans.

Account Enrollment and Automatic Investments

New ISSA customers should be able to establish an account in several ways: at a local brokerage branch, through an online web portal, or their employer at work. Once enrolled, an employee decides what percentage (1.0%-6.0%) of their net after-tax weekly (7-day) or bi-weekly (14-day) paycheck would be withheld as an elective payroll deduction. Customers may also select a specific dollar amount as a recurring contribution to their Privatized Social Security Account. Paystubs and W-2 forms would list current payroll cycles and cumulative contributions. An employer would process this transfer by sending cash funds (via bank wire or electronic funds transfer) to the retirement plan sponsor, who would automatically invest those funds in a timely manner.

ISSA Plan Income Restrictions and Contribution Limits

Maximum annual contribution limits and income restrictions on ISSA trust fund accounts would be the same as rules governing Roth IRA accounts, as of 2021. ISSA trust fund accounts would be available to adult US citizens (Age 18+) who have earned income. ISSA Account holders may contribute up to $6000 per year, or 100% of taxable income, whichever figure is less. Participants aged 50 and older may use the "catch-up" provision and contribute up to $7000 per year. However, no contributions may be made if adjusted gross income exceeds **$140,000** per year (single or head of household) or **$208,000** per year (married filing jointly). Contribution limits and income thresholds will adjust (through legislation) in future tax years. Like Roth IRA Accounts, ISSA Accounts are not available to married persons filing separately.

US Citizenship and Eligibility

As I mentioned earlier, ISSA trust fund accounts would be available to adult US citizens (Age 18+) who have earned income and are paying Social Security (FICA) taxes. This program was designed as a national retirement account for natural-born American citizens, US territory residents (American Samoa, Guam, Northern Mariana Islands, Puerto Rico, US Virgin Islands), and naturalized US citizens (as of December 31st, 2021) to invest in domestic US equity, bond and real estate funds. Ratification of the ISSA plan would directly support and fund the financial operations of the Social Security Administration and its long-term solvency as a US government agency. An unrestricted Social Security Number and card are necessary to enroll in an ISSA Account.

Closing Statement

This project began in July 2010 and was completed in July 2020 (10 years later). It is a tribute to the life, leadership, and Conservative legacy of former President Ronald Reagan. I secured the copyrights to this manuscript in 2021. In addition, a service mark application was also filed in 2021. Both forms of intellectual property could result in future royalty proceeds. Thank you for your time and interest in this plan.

Cordially,

Scott A Ginn

Mutual Fund Basics

Open-end mutual funds are among the most common and widely-used financial instruments in retirement accounts. These funds distribute virtually all of their income in the form of dividends and short or long-term capital gain distributions to their shareholders on a monthly, quarterly, semi-annual or annual basis. Although it is a fairly-simple investment, there are a few definitions that mutual fund investors should know.

1. net asset value (NAV): represents the market value of a group of stocks or bonds contained within a mutual fund on a per-share basis. Net asset values (NAVs) are calculated daily at the stock market close of business, or 4 PM (EST).
2. mutual fund exchange: a financial transaction to either buy into a mutual fund or sell out of a mutual fund, which requires a prospectus or written trade confirmation.
3. record date: the cutoff date used to determine which mutual fund shareholders are entitled to a distribution.
4. ex-dividend date: occurs 1 business day before the record date. Net asset values (NAVs) are calculated on this date, excluding declared dividend payments.
5. payable date: the date on which distributions are due, payable, and occur. The payable date usually takes place a few business days after the record date for mutual funds.

6. <u>Class A shares</u>: front-end sales load
7. <u>Class B shares</u>: contingent deferred sales charges
8. <u>Class C shares</u>: split-or level-sales load

Provisions in the ISSA plan do not restrict, impede or prevent free-market trading in any way. Active traders would simply need to pay for more (additional) transactions. This provision, and others, should conform to ERISA rules regarding frequent trading in individual plan accounts. The following illustration provides some criteria or basis for selection (inclusion) into the ISSA program.

Investment News: 100 Largest Mutual Fund Companies (2011)

Ranked by Retail Net Assets Under Management (AUM)

Rank	Fund Family	Retail Net AUM	Distinct Funds
2.	Fidelity Funds	$ 984 Billion	315
3.	American Funds	$ 956 Billion	42
4.	Franklin-Templeton Funds	$ 377 Billion	122
5.	T Rowe Price Funds	$ 345 Billion	110
10.	PIMCO Bond Funds	$ 118 Billion	73
12.	BlackRock Funds	$ 90 Billion	116
15.	MFS Funds	$ 71 Billion	74
24.	USAA Group Funds	$ 42 Billion	41
30.	Northern Trust Funds	$ 34 Billion	51
82.	Nationwide Mutual Funds	$ 8 Billion	30

2015 Organizational Update

When I began researching and writing this original business proposal in July of 2010, it was simply a concept; a rough draft, a 10-page assertion of how Privatized Social Security Accounts could work. Fast forward to July of 2020. The ISSA proposal is a completed 45-page blueprint of how Privatized Social Security Accounts can work.

Two major changes (within the Social Security Administration itself) have occurred during that period and are worthy of note. First, My SSA.gov online accounts were launched in January 2013. This new government web portal has 128-bit encryption, capable of handling secure financial transactions. Second, Social Security built its new National Support Center in Urbana, Maryland. Construction was completed in September of 2014. It was built to replace the aging facilities in Woodlawn, Maryland, and was expected to "handle the IT workload of the Agency for the next 20 years."

401(k) Plans, Vesting and In-Service Distributions

Privatized Social Security Accounts will have a formal, written booklet detailing their operation, account requirements, and key plan rules, similar to a 401(k) summary plan description (SPD). Unlike a 401(k) plan, there will be no minimum length of service requirements for eligibility. Eighteen will be the minimum age to enroll in an ISSA Account. Participation begins immediately, as is the time frame for when account holders begin to accumulate benefits and earn their rights, otherwise known as "vesting." In other words, contributions to (and earnings within) an ISSA Account will immediately become 100% vested. A 401(k) plan in-service rollover allows an employee (often at a specific age such as 55) to be able to roll their 401(k) plan into an IRA account while employed. Current tax law states that as long as a 401(k) plan participant is younger than 70 ½, an in-service distribution can be rolled over into a self-directed IRA account (A direct rollover would avoid mandatory 20% income tax withholding penalties and 10% early withdrawal penalties). However, to support the future viability of Privatized Social Security Accounts, Congress will need to determine whether 401(k) plan participants could perform an in-service distribution (IRA rollover) prior to age 59 ½, with the intent of replacing their workplace retirement plan. (There is no employer cost to include a 401(k) plan in-service rollover provision).

Upon opening an ISSA Account, the default portfolio will be a 2.0% contribution to the Merrill Lynch balanced fund until or unless a customer decides otherwise. If no investment preference is selected, this will be the default portfolio and default contribution rate. Mutual funds that will represent an asset class (based upon risk-adjusted performance) shall bid to occupy that premium webspace. Such funds could be called "best in class" or "featured funds," and will be negotiable. (As a new asset class, SRI-ESG mutual funds will be a basic, built-in ISSA plan investment option).

Operational Program Costs

In 2005, former President George W Bush's Full Social Security Privatization Plan would have required approval by Congress and cost American taxpayers (in borrowed costs) about $758 Billion Dollars to implement and operate (estimated).

In 2022 (and in contrast), My Partial Social Security Privatization Plan could startup with a total investment of $80 Million Dollars, or cost less than 1% of the former President's Social Security Privatization Plan (actual).

2017 Supplement: ERISA Rules and Dept of Labor Regulations

The regulatory framework of ERISA is worth mentioning. ERISA stands for the Employee Retirement Income Security Act of 1974. Title 1 of ERISA Act provisions establish minimum standards for operating private-sector employee benefit plans, namely retirement and pension plans. Furthermore, ERISA is administered by the Employee Benefits Security Administration (EBSA), a division of the Department of Labor. The 1975 Department of Labor IRA payroll deduction 'safe harbor' regulation clarified which plans were (or were not) subject to ERISA rules. Summarized, it states that a retirement plan will not be subject to Title 1 of the ERISA Act if 4 criteria are met:

1. The employer does not make contributions to the plan;
2. Employee participation is "completely voluntary";
3. The employer maintains minimal involvement in the retirement plan; <u>and</u>
4. The employer receives no direct compensation for offering the plan.

Therefore, according to the criteria mentioned above, my Independent Social Security Administration trust fund account, or ISSA Account, by its structure, composition, and function, should qualify as a non-ERISA account, or one which is not subject to Title 1 rules of the ERISA Act. Regarding the ISSA Account, existing tax laws and labor regulations already apply to two similar retirement plans: the non-ERISA 403(b) and Roth 403(b) accounts. Participants in 403(b) retirement plans include hospitals, public schools, religious and charitable organizations. According to the IRS, a 403(b) plan is a tax-sheltered annuity; contributions and investment earnings grow tax-deferred until retirement. A 1974 addition to the IRS Tax Code created 403(b) (7) custodial accounts, which allow participants to invest directly in mutual funds through a custodial account.

The Roth 403(b) account is an after-tax retirement plan; contributions and investment earnings grow tax-free until retirement. These accounts are offered through an employer and only by payroll deduction. Strict distribution rules apply to Roth 403(b) accounts. Withdrawals may be made tax-free only for "qualifying events": reaching the age of 59 ½, disability, death, separation from service, or financial hardship. Loans are available for Roth 403(b) retirement plans. Finally, required minimum distributions (RMDs) must begin at Age 70 ½ for Roth 403(b) accounts.

Related Acts: The Pension Protection Act of 2006

The Pension Protection Act of 2006 allows for automatic employee enrollment into a retirement plan, provided that a default portfolio and default contribution rate are specified. It protects employers (as fiduciaries) who offer such plans (called safe harbor investments), also known as qualified default investment alternatives. The QDIA must be a diversified mutual fund (to minimize the risk of large losses) and be:

1. A life-cycle or target-date retirement fund, or:
2. A balanced fund or asset-allocation fund.

(Effective 2008, the PPA and ERISA supercede any state laws which would directly prohibit automatic enrollment arrangements. Employees, however, may "opt-out" from enrolling into an elective Privatized Social Security Account).

Social Security Administration Overview

The Old-Age, Survivors and Disability Insurance (OASDI) program is a social insurance program administered by the Social Security Administration. Our nation's largest Entitlement program provides monthly benefits to qualified retired and disabled workers and their dependents and survivors of insured workers. The Social Security Administration is a federal government agency headquartered in Baltimore, Maryland, and became an independent government agency in 1995. More recently, construction of the SSA's modern National Support Center (datacenter) in Urbana, Maryland, was completed in September of 2014. A board of trustees is responsible for managing the OASDI trust funds (to be outlined below) and reporting annually to Congress on the financial and actuarial status of the trust funds. The board is comprised of six members; four of whom serve automatically by their positions in the federal government: the secretary of the Treasury, who is the managing trustee; the secretary of Labor, the secretary of the Department of Health and Human Services, and the commissioner of Social Security.

A person (worker) contributes to Social Security through either payroll taxes or self-employment taxes under the Federal Insurance Contributions Act (FICA) or the Self-Employed Contributions Act (SECA). These revenues are deposited into two trust funds: the Federal Old-Age and Survivor's Insurance Trust Fund (retirement component) and the federal Disability Insurance Trust Fund (disability component). Each program has its own trust fund to supply payments to its respective recipients. The revenues received by the trust funds can only be used to pay the benefits and operating expenses of the program. Our national debt is not paid for with Social Security taxes, but with money from the General Fund of the US Treasury, derived from personal income tax payments (74%), corporate income tax payments (15%), federal excise tax payments (2%), and other tax payments (9%). Such taxes are collected by the Internal Revenue Service (IRS). Social Security trust funds receive a credit equal to the Social Security payroll taxes deposited into the US Treasury by the IRS. The payroll taxes are allocated between the OASI and DI Trust Funds based on a proportion specified by law. As of 2019, they are (stated): **10.6%** for the OASI Trust Fund and **1.8%** for the DI Trust Fund. The far larger retirement program mentioned above is strictly a federal program. The smaller disability program, however, mandates federal-state cooperation (by law) to carry out the Disability Insurance (DI) program. State governments determine whether sufficient medical evidence exists to support a disabled person's ruling; costs are then reimbursed to the states by the federal government. The ISSA plan was built as a federal or national retirement account for employees of small to medium-sized firms (SMB Plan) who pay FICA taxes, but either lack any retirement plan at work; participate in a plan that does not offer employer-matching contributions, or contribute to a sub-standard 401(k) plan with high fees, expensive sales loads and poor investment options. Due to ISSA income restrictions and contribution limits, Congress will decide whether independent contractors and self-employed persons subject to the Self-Employed Contributions Act (SECA) may establish an ISSA Account. (The **2021** Annual Social Security Trustee Report projected that the OASI Trust Fund will be depleted in **2033**. Therefore, in my opinion, future ISSA plan revenues could be allocated between the OASI and DI Trust Funds, as Congress deems appropriate. Such market-based funding may assist the agency, and do the greatest good).

Mutual Fund Price List by NAV (July 31, 2016)

	Black Rock	Fidelity Funds	Franklin-Templeton	MFS Funds	Northern Trust	T Rowe Price	USAA Group
US Bond Fund	$10.83	$10.70	$ 8.41	$10.28	$10.02	$ 4.75	$10.08
Corporate Bond	$ 9.92	$11.70	$10.00	$14.32	$10.49	$ 9.92	$10.71
Total Bond Index	$10.46	$12.01	$10.11	$12.28	$10.95	$11.40	$13.40
Balanced Fund	$12.02	$22.21	$11.84	$18.27	$12.02	$22.27	$14.41
Utilities Fund	$21.07	$26.26	$18.66	$19.33	$12.37	$32.52	____
Real Estate Fund	$14.40	$17.26	$25.52	$17.16	$10.86	$31.05	____
Large-Cap Fund	$16.07	$27.44	$13.46	$26.60	$21.94	$20.32	$20.39
Mid-Cap Index	$10.23	$17.89	$14.76	$14.85	$17.76	$24.68	$17.29
Small-Cap Fund	$13.99	$17.85	$17.86	$10.81	$21.30	$42.15	$16.17
S&P 500 Index	$260.05	$76.51	$77.81	____	$26.37	$58.54	$31.03
International Fund	$11.90	$34.73	$13.68	$16.12	$ 9.58	$15.81	$26.89
Technology Fund	$16.76	$126.82	$50.43	$27.70	$21.63	$37.44	$22.03
SRI-ESG Fund (On 07/31/18)	$12.41	$22.45	$17.06	____	$10.54	____	____

ISSA Account Asset Levels and Fee Schedules

Account level	Free trades	Additional trades	Account value	Monthly service fees
Bronze	12	$26.00 per exchange	$0-$10,000	$32.00 per month ($384.00 per year)
Silver	24*	$26.00 per exchange	$10-$20,000	$28.00 per month ($336.00 per year)
Gold	24*	$26.00 per exchange	$20-$35,000	$24.00 per month ($288.00 per year)
Platinum	TBD	To Be Determined at A Later Date	More Than $35,000	$20.00 per month ($240.00 per year)

* Only no-load online mutual fund exchanges

Premium Investments For High Asset Accounts

<u>Bronze-level investors</u> have an account balance of $0-$10,000 and may invest only in basic investments and asset classes. No additional investments are offered.

<u>Silver-level investors</u> have an account balance of $10,000-$20,000 and have three additional investments to choose from. Class A, B, C shares (sales loads) are allowed.

1. Large-cap growth fund. Actively-managed Blue chip growth fund or Morningstar large-cap growth-only fund (not an index fund).
2. International stock fund (non-US foreign stocks). Developed markets fund; may hold limited emerging-markets stocks and Forex major market currencies. (e.g., Nationwide International Index Fund).
3. Healthcare sector fund. Fund may invest in biotechnology, pharmaceutical drug makers, medical equipment manufacturers, and healthcare providers (HMOs).

<u>Gold-level investors</u> have an account balance of $20,000-$35,000 and have six additional investments to choose from. Class A, B, C shares (sales loads) are allowed.

4. Technology sector fund. May be an actively-managed tech sector fund (e.g., T Rowe Price Science & Technology Fund) or a market-cap weighted tech index fund (e.g., USAA Nasdaq 100 Index Fund).
5. Commodities mutual fund. The fund invests in commodity derivatives, natural resources, and equity or bond holdings (not an index fund).
6. Global emerging markets fund. The fund invests in foreign emerging markets and Forex minor or exotic currencies. Diversified emerging markets stocks (e.g., Fidelity Emerging Markets Index Fund).

<u>Platinum-level investors</u> have an account balance of more than $35,000 and have the ability to invest in all of the funds listed previously, plus the possible future option of investing in a new asset class: exchange-traded funds (ETFs). Specifics to be determined at a later date.

Distinguished Carbon-Copy Recipients

The following members of Congress, government officials, business leaders, and news media experts have been sent a recent copy (or prior version) of this original manuscript:

1. Paul Ryan (R-WIS), former US Speaker of the House of Representatives
2. Kevin McCarthy (R-CA), House Minority Leader
3. Dr. Ben Bernanke, chairman of the Federal Reserve Board of Governors
4. Senator John McCain (R-AZ), chairman of Senate Armed Services Committee
5. John Boehner (R-OH), former US Speaker of the House of Representatives
6. Senator Mitch McConnell (R-KY), Senate Majority Leader
7. Brian Riedl, senior fellow at The Manhattan Institute
8. Mark Meadows (R-NC), chairman of the House Freedom Caucus
9. William H Gross, founder of PIMCO Global Investments
10. Dr. Alan Greenspan, chairman of the Federal Reserve Board of Governors
11. Dan Crenshaw (R-TX), US House Representative, former Navy SEAL

First Revision

1. Senator Mitt Romney (R-UT), former governor of Massachusetts, 2012 Republican Presidential Candidate
2. Newt Gingrich (R-GA), former US Speaker of the House of Representatives, 2012 Republican Presidential Candidate
3. Congressman Ron Paul (R-TX), 2012 Republican Presidential Candidate

Second Revision

1. Senator Marco Rubio (R-FL), 2016 Republican Presidential Candidate
2. Senator Ted Cruz (R-TX), 2016 Republican Presidential Candidate
3. Governor Gary Johnson (L-NM), 2016 Libertarian Presidential Candidate

Distinguished Business Organization, Academic Institution and Research Institute Recipients
(December 2015)

1. Arthur C Brooks, former president of the American Enterprise Institute (AEI)
2. Edwin A Finn, editor and president of Barron's Magazine
3. Michael Grebe, former president and CEO of the Bradley Foundation
4. John Engler, former president of Corporate Business Roundtable (BRT)
5. Edward H Crane, founder and president emeritus of the CATO Institute
6. Michael A Branham, former president of the Certified Financial Planner Board (CFP)
7. Senator Jim DeMint, former president of the Heritage Foundation
8. Dr. Larry P Arnn, president of Hillsdale College
9. Charles Koch, founder of the Charles Koch Charitable Foundation
10. Brian Riedl, senior fellow at the Manhattan Institute
11. Dan Danner, president of the National Federation of Independent Business (NFIB)
12. Reince Priebus, former chairman of the Republican National Committee (RNC)
13. Thomas J Donahue, former president and CEO of the US Chamber of Commerce

POSTSCRIPT

As I update this section in February of 2022, I'd like to briefly expand on the reasons why I began writing in the first place. Capitalism can be a force for good, not greed. Congressional spending and debt accumulation, authorized by all Presidential administrations in the 21ˢᵗ century, dwarfs that of anything seen before in our nation's history and continues to this day. At the turn of the last century, at the end of fiscal year 2000, our gross national debt was **5.674 Trillion** dollars. As of this writing, in February of 2022, our gross national debt is **30 Trillion** dollars and counting. Mainly for political reasons, our major Entitlement programs have been neglected to the brink of insolvency. I have focused on only one of these programs: Social Security. Wealthier individuals already have access to tax-advantaged investments (municipal and Treasury bond funds) and tax-free accounts (Roth IRAs) and can afford to hire accountants and wealth-management firms to file their taxes and manage their investments. The ISSA Account was designed to benefit working-class employees (at small-to medium-size businesses) who either lack access to any retirement plan at work, would like an alternative to the 401(k) plan, or just want the opportunity to invest tax-free like the experts already do.

I felt it was important to be as thorough as possible, to show people a concrete plan of how Capitalism can improve the quality of people's lives through their own efforts. My goal is simple and direct: turning this manuscript into a functioning government program. This wouldn't be easy; complexity is a reason why this type of account has never been presented to Congress before, let alone voted on. And the ISSA plan would likely require an Act of Congress. In addition, it would require cooperation and agreements between the federal government and Wall Street; on a scale never attempted before. Regardless, in my view, the youngest American Generations deserve nothing less than their own Privatized Social Security Account.

November 2020
ISSA Business Contract

To Brian Moynihan, President and CEO of Bank of America-Merrill Lynch:

Hello Sir, my name is Scott A Ginn. I have been working on a business concept regarding Privatized Social Security Accounts for the last 10 years. After substantial and numerous revisions, it is now complete. My idea is a grassroots conservative Republican concept and an issue which is important to three American Generations: Generation X, Millennium Generation, and Generation Z. Quite simply, younger generations do not trust government promises of future benefits; are skeptical of the agency's future solvency and want Privatized Social Security Accounts of their own. I firmly believe that entitlement reform is critical to ensure our nation's future; my 45-page manuscript describes (in detail) how Privatized Social Security Accounts can work without harming seniors or incurring massive costs.

I am proposing a new, actively-managed no-load mutual fund marketplace, which only includes for-profit investment companies. This would be a government account but run by the private sector: a Privatized Roth Social Security Account. Your company has the scale and IT infrastructure (customer service phone coverage, local branch banks and regional investor centers, new account processing capacity, web integration, and brokerage operations) necessary to run a program as large as I have formulated. This concept would likely need approval by Congress, the Securities and Exchange Commission, and the Social Security Administration, respectively.

Two main sources of new revenue would originate from ISSA Account operations and are actually fees: monthly account maintenance fees and frequent trading penalties or fees. To write this business plan, I had to "stand in the shoes" of the federal government, at times, to strike a balance at what would be fair and reasonable for all stakeholders: the retirement plan sponsor or provider, investment companies offering their mutual funds in a new marketplace, employees (investors), small and medium-sized businesses offering the ISSA plan, and the Social Security Administration itself.

For instance, my decision to provide a minimal number of free annual mutual fund exchanges was intentional. In my view, the government should not incentivize (or encourage) unlimited trading in a retirement account. In addition, broker-dealers already offer generous free trades to new retail clients; the ISSA plan would not compete against them in this regard. The conservative nature of basic investments offered in the ISSA plan is also an example of fair, reasonable, and suitable policymaking. Therefore, I propose a revenue-sharing agreement between Bank of America and the federal government. Account maintenance fees are simply a "cost of doing business" in the banking, brokerage, and credit industries and are quite common. Regardless, they provide the financial services firm with a stable, predictable operational revenue stream.

ISSA Monthly Account Maintenance Fee Revenue-Sharing Table

Bronze-level: $0-$10,000	$16.00 Social Security	+	$16.00 Brokerage firm	=	$32.00/Month
Silver-level: $10-$20,000	$14.00 Social Security	+	$14.00 Brokerage firm	=	$28.00/Month
Gold-level: $20-$35,000	$12.00 Social Security	+	$12.00 Brokerage firm	=	$24.00/Month
Platinum-level: Over $35,000	$10.00 Social Security	+	$10.00 Brokerage firm	=	$20.00/Month

For extra or additional mutual fund exchanges, however, I believe that a compromise should be made. ISSA investors are given a flat number of free, annual mutual fund exchanges by account balances: bronze level (12), silver level (24), gold level (24), and platinum level (TBD). They could be evenly distributed throughout the year, and allocated by calendar month.

Proposed Free ISSA Mutual Fund Exchange Table

Account level	Number of free mutual fund exchanges	Frequency
Bronze	1	Monthly
Silver	2	Monthly
Gold	2	Monthly
Platinum	TBD	Monthly

(Any unused free mutual fund exchanges will not roll over to the next month).

Instead of mutual fund transaction fees, all exchanges beyond these monthly allotments will be charged $26.00 per additional online exchange. Your firm would receive $23.00 of these extra fees; Social Security would receive $3.00 per transaction. I arrived at this pricing structure based on late 2017 costs of mutual fund exchanges by online discount brokers in the industry. Your proprietary platform Merrill Edge (Bank of America/Merrill Lynch), for example, charges $20.00 for no-load, transaction fee mutual fund exchanges; E-Trade (acquired by Morgan Stanley in 2020) also charged $20.00 per transaction. Scottrade (acquired by TD Ameritrade in 2018) charged less, at $17.00 for online mutual fund exchanges. Due to the inherent power, size, and resources of the federal government and an agency such as the Social Security Administration, I recommend that Bank of America charge $26.00 for additional ISSA mutual fund exchanges, thereby not under-pricing industry discount brokers. The original ISSA institutional account structure was designed for competition; to separate investment functions between several companies with specialized expertise.

This view has changed over time. Since Bank of America is both an investment bank and broker-dealer, which can settle its own transactions (and those of its competitors), I have concluded it would be the most efficient and cost-effective if Bank of America handled the entire transaction. Bank of America would serve as the investment bank and execute the mutual fund exchange; clear and settle the transaction, credit or debit the customer's required Merrill Lynch money market mutual fund, and send out a trade confirmation to the shareholder address of record (or e-mail address).

This level of involvement comes at a price, however. I believe that this business plan is worth $25-$35 million dollars; however, this figure is negotiable. Bank of America would be granted the exclusive rights to use, offer, and promote the ISSA Account and ISSA plan to customers. These rights may include any intellectual property rights (copyrights, a trademark, patent, or service mark) originating from this business concept and proposal. This sum of money ($25-$35 million dollars) would be deducted from the $80 million dollars we would ask Congress to grant to Bank of America as startup capital for website construction, advertising, promotion, legal, regulatory, and other business costs associated with the formation of the ISSA Account. Formal letters of interest would need to be sent to the 10 investment companies I have expertly selected to see if they are interested in participating in the ISSA marketplace. They would have to agree to the terms and conditions set forth in the enclosed business plan.

(I cannot re-create this paragraph from either memory or records. Since it contains specific contract language describing the terms of a reciprocal services agreement, Republican Senate Majority Leader Mitch McConnell's delivered final version of this plan shall remain; with the following numbers substituted) (replaced):

Contract duration:	10 years (no change)
Estimated contract value:	$100-$300 million per year (revised)

For the ISSA plan, I would like Bank of America to waive any annual account low balance fee policies; ISSA investors will have smaller account balances than retail customers, as it should take a number of years for their accounts to grow in value. 'Modest, infrequent and equivalent' increases in mutual fund trading costs will be the standard; and allowed after one full calendar year of operations. In addition, I would like ISSA investors to be able to use the Merrill Edge Guided Investing Program, modified for mutual fund investing; the $5,000 minimum investment threshold could remain.

Finally, most major banks and brokerage firms all charge at least $50.00 for short-term redemption fees on the sale of mutual funds owned less than 90 days. For the ISSA Account, I would like Bank of America to reduce this amount and charge no more than $30.00 for short-term redemption fees, if possible. I would encourage Bank of America to negotiate with participating mutual fund companies to limit, reduce or eliminate such fees on certain funds offered in this plan.

Bank of America would have to lobby Congress in support of this idea, of course. Such legislation could be entitled, "The Social Security Privatization and Modernization Act of 2022." My relationship or role with Bank of America would have to be determined at some point: as a business partner or consultant, Bank of America employee (Project Manager-Privatized Social Security Accounts), or government contractor. Thank you for your time, and I welcome interest or feedback.

Sincerely,
Scott A Ginn